Mollye and Cam,
We wish you a Merry Christmas and many blessings in 2012!
Much love,
Helen & Ridley

Blessings,
2010

Secret of the Pearls

written & illustrated by

rochelle frazier

To my Sweeteas,

HollandRose, Alexis,
Ashley & Addison

May you always cherish
your southern roots!

I love you,
MommaRo

text & illustration copyright ©2009 by rochelle frazier
sweeteas is a registered trademark of rochelle frazier designs, llc
printed in the united states . chase bridges press . first edition .
isbn 978-0-9816108-1-8
www.thesweeteas.com

Well, I do declare,

look at all these precious girls!

I think they've returned to learn the

"Secret of the Pearls."

This is a special day. One you'll treasure most!

You'll become an "official" sweetea,

and we are delighted to be your host.

So please gather closely, we must start without delay.

For there is much to learn before we send you on your way.

By now you know we start with

how do you do?

Today you are grand, so

kisses

you get too!!

In honor of you

a tea we will share,

to pass on the letters only we

sweeteas

proudly wear.

Now, since this is such a memorable day for you,
your momma, grand & mimi,
well, they are all invited too!

this also includes...

Yayas, Girlies & Ronos

just the same!

those who "love you to pieces,"
no matter what "grandma" name they claim .

Of course, a
Sweetea
takes pride in looking her very best,
'cause like momma says,

"Honey, ya just never know when

you'll end up in the local press."

So I've asked
Cutie Pie & Princess
to prepare you for your
Sweetea debute.

they are what we call the

"fashionistas" of our lil' crew!

We'll fetch your favorite

party dress,

and of course, your

fancy pearls!

then we'll grab your most

adorable hat,

to impress the other

girls.

We'll add some flowers, ribbon, and a splash or two of color,

and we'll curl up your precious hair to awe your

dear grandmother!

Now that you are a

"Princess"

in your best tea party attire,

you can add some lil' white gloves, but it's

absolutely not required.

Some would say

"Less is certainly more,"

and others, like our dear Princess,

would bedazzle you

to the floor!

What's most important is that your own
personality shines through!
It's essential that you know, we
Sweeteas

love You

for just being

Now it's time to take our places,
so we may begin our tea,
we'll turn it over to Angel, our lil'
Miss Southern Hospitality.

thank you for joining our first "official"

Sweet "tea!"

We truly need your help to
uphold and share our
southern legacy!

First, I must thank Sunshine for our
delicious treats!!

She surely has prepared the perfect
Sweetea feast!

Now, if honey or milk you so desire for your tea,
you may raise your spoon to our hostess, Baby & Sweet Pea!

Well, you must be wondering what in heavens is the

Secret of the Pearls?

It's something very special shared between a southern momma and her girls.

To:
My Sweetea

I thank my God everytime I think of you
♡ Mom

It starts with learning that beauty comes from the bottom of your heart!!!

It's our charm & character

that sets us southern girls apart.

It's like we have a lil' magic to get the things we need.

the secret is...

to slowly bat your eyes, while asking,

"May I Pretty Please?"

This especially works on
Daddies & Papas, you will find.

the **Secret** is.....

they will give you the **world** for some

A good southern girl also knows to respect her elders.

It's just part of our upbring to practice our best southern manners.

sts

It's simply yes ma'am,

yes sir, thank you and pretty please.

Of course, "God Bless You" when you hear your neighbor sneeze.

The secret is...people will go a lil' out of their way,

if you use a touch of kindness in the common things you say.

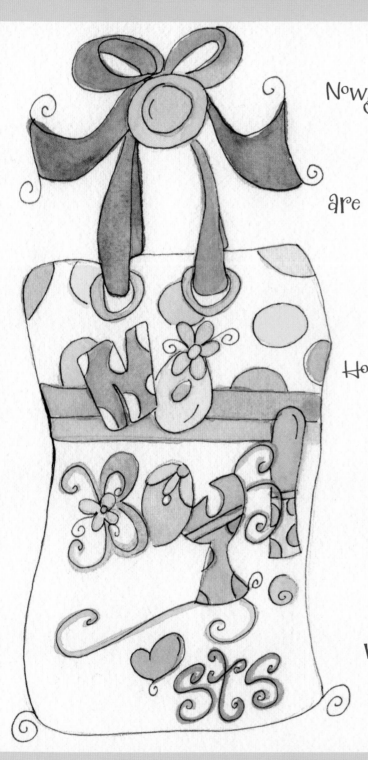

Now, you must know that the only boys
that get half our time,
are those that run up and down the
Sweetea family line.

However, there will come a time when

suitors fare your way

the **secret** is....

Your **southern drawl**

will melt their hearts away.

So sughar, always remember to use your
gift of southern birth!
Be proud to say, "I'm from...

Alanna,
S'vanah or Dallas...
Foat Wuth!

Now, despite what the current magazines or "trends" may say, there are certain rules we Southern girls must learn to always obey!!

the **secret** is...

"Bless your heart," you are certain to hear...

if you are found wearing white at particular times of the year.

But the heart of the
secrets that we *Sweeteas* embrace,
like a precious pearl, we represent
style, elegance, and grace.
We have both beauty and strength to stand alone,
but when we're strung together our bond is fahevah strong!

As you may know,

pearls come in many ways;

some are natural & some are made.

So no matter how far from the

south your birth place

may be,

we can still nurture you into the

most charming

Sweetea!

So we open our door and welcome you in,

'cause it's just good southern hospitality

to make strangers feel like kin.

Sweeteas
1204 cupcake cove
magnolia, ms 39652

Now, if what we have shared has touched your heart,

and you and yours would like to take part,

then raise your pinky and repeat after me.

I, _(your name)_, promise to

uphold and share the

Creed of the Sweeteas!

To be the best friend a friend could ever be,
and never get too old to sit on my
daddy's knee.
To always take to heart my
momma's best advice,
"Pretty is as Pretty does,"
so before I act,
I'll think twice!!

To share

faith, hope, & love

with those who cross my path,

and appreciate the simple gifts of

bedtime stories and bubble baths.

To dance like no one's watching, and to follow my dreams,

because I know in my heart, if

" Ye ask believing, Ye shall receive!!"

To know that I am special, just 'cause I'm **ME**,

and to share these treasured **secrets** with those

deserving of being

Sweeteas.

I am a pearl.

I'm a precious Sweetea!

I promise to

uphold and share my

Southern legacy!

Now that you know the magic held by us southern girls,

we gladly give you our letters to compliment your pearls.

there's one more

before you go,

that we sweeteas think it's

essential you know!!!

there will certainly be those that criticize your
sweet southern ways,
but a Sweetea says....

"Bless her heart,"
and simply turns away, because it's

No   Secret

WE'D *all* BE IN A MUCH BETTER PLACE...

The Story Behind The Sweeteas

It seems that lately I have heard so many stories of sadness and heartbreak from friends and family. In times like these, we often wonder what good will come from this suffering. I feel it's very important to also share stories of blessings and God's grace, and hopefully proof that "good does come from bad," so I have decided to share my story with you.

The Sweeteas were born in Spring of 2006, after the birth of my twin boys, Houston & Jackson. I had a very difficult pregnancy post Katrina, and I ultimately found myself at 31 years old in congestive heart failure. Fearing for my life and the future for my children, I prayed without ceasing for healing and inspiration. I was told that I would most likely not return to work, so I prayed even more for one great idea that would change my life, so I could support my family. It was almost immediaté that I found myself writing and drawing about these cast of characters that were

"touching the world with their Southern Grace".

It was surely the inspiration that I had been praying for, because today, I am healthy, I have a beautiful family, and I have faith that has moved many mountains from my path . I get the opportunity to read this sweet book to children all over the South, and it brings me more joy than I can possibly share in words to receive emails from little girls and their moms about how Sweeteas touches their hearts. Had I not been through so much suffering in 2006, I would not have Sweeteas to share with you today.

I pray that all who read this book will see it as an example of the goodness that can come from unwaivering faith!
Blessings to y'all,
Rochelle

In loving memory of a "true" Sweetea, Susan Haskins

thanks

To my loving family
Holland Rose, Houston, & Jackson
Papa, Roro, Kit, Keri, & Addie Rae
I love y'all to pieces!!!!

To my Mom
Thank you for never leaving my side.
I couldn't have made it without you.

To Those Who Lift Me Up!
Kelsey, Kristy, Lori, Christine, Ruth & Darla

To the Most Wonderful Godmothers to My Children
JJ, Aunt Rose, Aunt Jane & Cherie

To Thomas & Teresa
I would never finish this without your help!!

www.thesweeteas.com

I thank my God everytime
I think of you!
Rochelle